KU-158-794

BERNARD SHAW

BERNARD SHAW

by

A. C. WARD

PUBLISHED FOR
THE BRITISH COUNCIL
BY LONGMAN GROUP LTD

LONGMAN GROUP LTD
Longman House, Burnt Mill, Harlow, Essex

Associated companies, branches and representatives throughout the world

First published 1950
Revised editions 1951, 1957, 1960, 1963, 1966
Reprinted with minor amendments and additions to Bibliography 1970

Printed in Great Britain by
F. Mildner & Sons, London, EC1

R. ISBN 0582010012

BERNARD SHAW

In length, productiveness, and influence the career of Bernard Shaw is unparalleled in the history of modern literature. His first printed words—a letter commenting critically on a religious mission in Dublin conducted by the American evangelists Dwight L. Moody and Ira D. Sankey—appeared in *Public Opinion*, a London weekly, on 3 April 1875, when he was nineteen. His regular career as a writer started in 1885, when he became a book reviewer to the London *Pall Mall Gazette*. From that date for more than sixty years he continued to be active as a critic, mainly in other fields than that of books: of art, of music, of the theatre, and (chiefly) of public affairs. From 1879 to 1883 he was an unsuccessful novelist; from 1892 onwards a dramatist, the most notable of the period.

He had left Dublin in 1876 and settled in London, but his first box-office success in the theatre was with the New York production by Richard Mansfield of *The Devil's Disciple* in 1897. This made it possible for him to marry in the next year, at the age of forty-two. In London his early plays had caused much discussion, most of it unfavourable, and the third of them, *Mrs Warren's Profession* (written 1893-4), was banned by the British censor [1] from the public stage until 1926, though it was produced in the United States in 1905 and at a private performance in London by the Stage Society in 1902.

British prejudice against his plays began to break down in 1905, when King Edward VII attended a performance of *John Bull's Other Island* at the Royal Court Theatre, Sloane Square, London, during a repertory season under the financial management of J. E. Vedrenne with H. Granville Barker as producer.[2] That Vedrenne-Barker season from 1904 to 1907 has become famous in the annals of the English

[1] See below, p. 29.

[2] For details see: *The Court Theatre 1904-1907. A Commentary and a Criticism*, by Desmond MacCarthy. With an Appendix containing Reprinted Programmes (1907).

stage, for it established a new type of play and a new style of acting and stage-production.[1] It led the London theatre-going public to accept and to become familiar with the discussion of serious subjects such as politics and religion, with restrained performances by the players, and with naturalistic stage décor. Until then, the British theatre had been for more than a century dominated by unreality both in the topics and in the language of the plays as well as in the acting and scenery. The standards of the theatre throughout the nineteenth century had caused the word 'theatrical' to be applied to behaviour and surroundings bearing no resemblance to ordinary people's experience of life. In the plays produced during the Court Theatre season a determined and successful effort was made to close the gap between life and the theatre; and although the example then set has often since been ignored, the British stage has never sunk back entirely into former artificial ways. But Bernard Shaw's naturalism was of a strictly limited kind. Though his plays treat of serious themes rooted in living human experience, they are the work of a man in whom aesthetic sensibility was hereditary—his mother's life was given up to music—and in whom it was also fostered by the circumstances of his upbringing. He was a master of superb rhetoric which at times assumes the tones of poetry; yet it is never more than suppressed poetry, since Shaw's lifelong abhorrence of the romantic attitude imposed a studied restraint upon his instinctive emotional urgency. Throughout his public life he played the part of a man in a mask, so much so that it was easy for his detractors to represent him as an ogre with a heart of stone. It is the rhetoric, the suppressed poetry, as well as the fundamental humanity and the abounding wit, that lifts his plays in spirit and temper from the plane of naturalism to that of high comedy; and it is as high comedy that they must be acted on the stage: comedy which is an

[1] Shaw's idiosyncratic view, however, was that there was nothing 'new' in all this, but that he and Barker and Gilbert Murray were reviving the classical school of Euripides and Shakespear, Goethe and Ibsen.

illuminating commentary on life, not simply a naturalistic mirrored reflection of it. 'My plays', he wrote, 'are no more economic treatises than Shakespear's, . . . all my plays were written . . . as plays of life, character, and human destiny like those of Shakespear or Euripides'.[1]

As a playwright on that level he had been accepted by the time the Court Theatre season ended in 1907. In the three years or so through which it lasted, eleven of Shaw's plays had been given a total of 701 performances. Among them was the first of his masterpieces, *Man and Superman* (written 1901–3; published 1903; first performed 1905), the third act of which contains the earliest complete statement of what he afterwards came to call his religion of Creative Evolution, the main theme of his life-work.

Even those who by 1905 had recognized Shaw as the outstanding British dramatist of his generation, continued for many years to question the likelihood of his taking a permanent place in literature. It was doubted that his plays would retain their interest when the problems treated in them—slums, prostitution, women's rights, marriage customs, etc.—had ceased to be of immediate concern. Such doubts have since been set aside by successive revivals. When *You Never Can Tell*, first performed in 1899, was revived in London half a century later, it drew larger audiences and for a longer period than at any time before. It was more surprising to find that *Widowers' Houses* (1892), a cruder play and more topical to its original date, still had a lively interest for audiences in the late twentieth century. In 1965, after another kind of 'new' drama had flooded the English-speaking theatres in the wake of the Second World War, a series of simultaneously successful Shaw revivals was headed by an Edinburgh Festival production of *Too True to Be Good*, which had been coldly received when it first appeared in 1932. Transferred to London from Scotland, the new production long outstayed the intended 'limited run', and impressed a new generation of audiences by the

[1] 'Biographers' Blunders Corrected': *Sixteen Self Sketches* (1949), p. 89.

prophetic quality of this voice from the 1930s which was still disturbingly undated in the 1970s. It irrupted with force into the atomic age which shattered traditional beliefs and, in current drama, bred the life-denying modes of 'the theatre of the absurd' and 'the theatre of cruelty'. In the final speech of *Too True to Be Good* Aubrey Bagot asks: 'Are we any the less obsessed with a belief when we are denying it than when we are affirming it?' and he adds: 'I must have affirmations to preach. Without them the young will not listen to me; for even the young grow tired of denials.' However much the new wave of interest in Shaw may have betokened a hunger for affirmations in an age of denials—the satanic Everlasting Nay—it also represented the rediscovery of Shaw as a wit and humorist who could contemplate disaster with moral courage and spiritual buoyancy.

Those who consider Bernard Shaw's work as a whole, and in relation to his tireless crusade for social justice and righteousness and the intellectual enlightenment he generated and spread abroad, can have little doubt that he belongs to the ages and with the immortals. Sophocles died at ninety, Shakespear[1] at fifty-two, Lope de Vega at sixty-three, Molière at fifty-one, Goldoni at eighty-six, Tchekov at forty-four, Ibsen at seventy-eight, Tolstoy at eighty-two. In his nineties Shaw was still writing for the living theatre, turning for the first time to the composition of a puppet play, and maintaining with mental vigour his passionate and seemingly inexhaustible concern with public affairs. While he fell short of the prodigious output of Lope de Vega for the stage, the stage was but one among several fields of Shavian activity: 'For every play I have written I have made hundreds of speeches and published big books on Fabian Socialism. There is behind my plays a thought-out sociology. . . .' Those speeches and those big books were

[1] There is no agreed spelling of Shakespear's name, which varies even in his own signatures to documents. Shaw's preferred spelling is used throughout this booklet, though most modern British writers add a final e.

assimilated into the mind of his generation and it is possible that the future will give little conscious heed to them. Even in the author's lifetime the big books, except as monuments of English prose by one of the great masters of English prose, were regretted by some as time-absorbing hindrances to further plays that Shaw might have written.

But beyond the speeches and the big books, beyond the plays and their prefaces, there was the man himself: the man of whom G. K. Chesterton said, 'this shall be written of our time: that when the spirit who denies besieged the last citadel, blaspheming life itself, there were some, there was one especially, whose voice was heard and whose spear was never broken'.[1] Shaw was for modern Britain what Socrates was for ancient Greece; and in a sense which the Greeks would have understood he may well appear in the perspective of history as the Good Man of his time.

I

George Bernard Shaw was born in Ireland on 26 July 1856 at 3 Upper Synge Street (now 33 Synge Street), Dublin, the third and youngest child and only son of George Carr Shaw and Lucinda Elizabeth Shaw (*née* Gurly). His father was second cousin to a petty noble (a baronet), and as 'the youngest son of a younger son of a younger son' he inherited aristocratic tendencies which he lacked money to gratify; for, under the British system of inheritance at the time, property passed to eldest sons and left younger sons impoverished. Lucinda Gurly, the daughter of a country gentleman, married in spite of warnings of her bridegroom's frequent drunkenness and in ignorance of his lack of the practical ability required for the maintenance of a wife and family.

Until 1850 George Carr Shaw held a sinecure office as a civil servant in the Four Courts (the Department of Justice) in Dublin. In that year, his office having been abolished,

[1] In *George Bernard Shaw* (1910).

he was retired with a pension, which he sold in order to invest the money in an unsuccessful corn-merchant's business. Bernard Shaw therefore grew up in an atmosphere of genteel impecuniosity which he described as more humiliating than the life of the born poor who have no social standing or cultural background to maintain. His family were, he says, 'downstarts'—those who gravitate depressingly downward in the social scale—as distinct from the 'upstarts' who have the invigorating experience of climbing away from the bottom levels.

After rudimentary lessons from a private governess and some instruction in Latin given by his uncle-in-law, Bernard Shaw was sent in 1867 to the Dublin Wesleyan Connexional School (a Protestant non-sectarian institution which has since become Wesley College), and later to a private school in the country. He said he learnt nothing, and in 1869 he was transferred to the Central Model Boys' School in Dublin attended mostly by Roman Catholic children of the trading class. He remembered this experience as 'an episode in my boyhood formerly so repugnant to me that for eighty years I never mentioned it to any mortal creature, not even to my wife. It was to me what the blacking warehouse was to Dickens.'[1] The sense of shame thus generated came from the fact that Ireland was then ruled by Protestant England, with a Protestant Viceroy and Viceregal Court installed in Dublin. Protestantism was consequently synonymous with social and political eminence and Catholicism with social and political inferiority. Though Shaw recognized at an early age the absurdity and injustice of this assumption of superiority by an alien minority, and freed himself from its falsity so far as his own conduct and convictions were implicated, the psychological effect of being forced to mix at school with a despised class branded him with an emotional scar which rational thinking failed to clear away until he had passed the age of ninety, although he was at the Model School for no more than eight months. He then went

[1] 'Shame and Wounded Snobbery': *Sixteen Self Sketches*, p. 20.

for the last two years of his school life to the Dublin English Scientific and Commercial Day School, leaving in 1871.

Meanwhile, his mother had lost interest as well as faith in her husband, and turned for consolation to the development of her remarkable singing voice. Her music teacher, George John Vandaleur Lee,[1] became important in Bernard Shaw's life when the family moved into Lee's house in 1868. During the next four years the boy was surrounded by musical people constantly rehearsing Italian and German operas and oratorios, which he came to know as thoroughly as young people later came to know 'pop' tunes. Not only did this informal musical education provide the grounding which qualified him to become a music critic in London years afterwards, but it also affected his plays in a marked manner. Their orchestral and operatic quality[2] (which none of Shaw's 'realistic' imitators was able to reproduce) is most apparent in Act III of *Man and Superman*. It is not without significance, also, that *Arms and the Man* was utilized as the basis for the libretto of a popular light opera, *The Chocolate Soldier*,[3] while some years after his death *Pygmalion* was adapted as *My Fair Lady*, one of the most successful of all musical comedies. In those early Dublin days, too, he acquired (at the National Gallery of Ireland) a knowledge of painting and sculpture sufficient to enable him to practise as an art critic from 1886 to 1889.

Most writers on Shaw have taken proper account of the part which art and, particularly, music played in his youth, but little attention has been given to his love of nature.[4]

[1] Though Shaw spelt the middle name as above, it was correctly 'Vandeleur'. See John O'Donovan: *Shaw and the Charlatan Genius* (1965).

[2] In an article, 'Rules for Play Producers' (*Strand Magazine*, London, July 1949), Shaw said that the chief actors should be selected with attention to voice contrast: 'The four principals should be soprano, alto, tenor, and bass.'

[3] Shaw insisted that the programmes should describe this as 'an unauthorized parody' of his play.

[4] In *Shaw* (1949) C. E. M. Joad drew a false conclusion from his mistaken statement that Shaw's attitude 'from one end of the plays to the other rigorously excludes nature and all mention of nature' (p. 227).

A note written in 1947 dwells upon the delight he felt at the age of ten when he went to live at 'Torca Cottage, high on Dalkey Hill, commanding views of Dublin Bay . . . with a vast and ever-changing expanse of sea and sky far below and far above. . . . I had only to open my eyes there to see such pictures as no painter could make for me. I could not believe that such skies existed anywhere else in the world until I read Shakespear's "this majestical roof fretted with golden fire", and wondered where he could have seen it if not from Torca Cottage. The joy of it has remained with me all my life.'[1] There is a reflection of this joy in the opening scene of *The Apple Cart* (1930) when Sempronius says: 'I should have been as happy as a man in a picture gallery looking at the dawns and sunsets, the changing seasons, the continual miracle of life ever renewing itself. Who could be dull with pools in the rocks to watch?' And in *Too True to Be Good* The Patient revels in 'the delicious dawns, the lovely sunsets, the changing winds, the cloud pictures, the flowers, the animals and their ways, the birds and insects and reptiles'.

When Shaw left school in 1871 he went to work as junior clerk for a Dublin estate agent. His wage was eighteen shillings a month; his duties included the filing of incoming letters, the press-copying of outgoing ones, the keeping of the postage account, and, in the role of errand boy, buying lunch for his fellow clerks. Lunch at that time, he says, was not a serious meal: his own was a penny roll of bread. After about a year, by which time his wage had become forty shillings a month, the post of cashier fell vacant and Shaw was appointed temporarily to fill it. Giving complete satisfaction, he was retained and his pay increased to four pounds a month. His fellow clerks—'gentlemen apprentices'—received no salary; they were mostly university graduates paying a premium to be taught the estate agency business. They tried, unsuccessfully, to argue Shaw back into belief

[1] 'Am I an Educated Person?': *Sixteen Self Sketches*, p. 72.

in Protestant Christianity (while still a young boy he had renounced orthodox religion but had experienced that 'dawning of moral passion' described by John Tanner in Act I of *Man and Superman*[1]); while Shaw taught them to sing operatic arias in the office. He remained in that office through four and a half years, and when he left in 1876 to migrate to London he was given a testimonial certifying that he was 'a young man of great business capacity, strict accuracy, and thoroughly reliable and trustworthy. Anything given him to do was always accurately and well done.'[2]

In the preceding year his mother and sisters had also left Dublin for London, where Mrs Shaw set up as a teacher of singing, preserving also her own perfectly produced voice until her death in 1913 at the age of eighty-three.

II

The far greater purchasing value of money in the 1870s as compared with that in our time made Shaw's pay as clerk and cashier less of a pittance than it seems today. Even so, it was not a living wage and he had to depend upon his father to supplement it. His determination to leave the estate office, however, had more than a monetary cause. His employer, Charles Townshend, had drawn from him a pledge to refrain from religious controversy in working hours. Shaw gave the promise hesitantly, and, feeling that it was an intolerable restraint upon his freedom of conscience, decided that an office career would be impossible for him. His mother's departure for London served as a strong incentive to follow her example, but it was not the sole motive, nor the originating one. 'London was the literary centre for the English language, and for such artistic

[1] See also the autobiographical Preface to his first novel, *Immaturity*, which remained unpublished until 1930.

[2] See *In Praise of Bernard Shaw*, edited by Allan M. Laing (1949), p. 10.

culture as the realm of the English language (in which I proposed to be king) could afford.'[1]

A king of language he was at length to become, but his kingdom was at that time afar off and it was not until twenty years later that he could presume to say 'My destiny was to educate London'. In the nine years from 1876 to 1885 his pen earned him no more than six pounds fifteen shillings for an article, five shillings for a set of verses, and five pounds for a commissioned essay, ordered by a friendly solicitor, on patent medicines.[2] For support during that period he depended in part upon a weekly allowance of one pound from his father (who remained in Ireland and died in 1885), but mainly upon his mother, with whom he lived at 13 Victoria Grove (now Netherton Grove), Fulham Road, in south-west London. It was no doubt with a sharp remembrance of his own state of mind that, later, he made Tanner say in *Man and Superman* (Act I): 'The true artist will let his wife starve, his children go barefoot, his mother drudge for his living at seventy, sooner than work at anything but his art.' For a few months in 1879 he worked for the Edison Telephone Company in the City of London, and in that year also wrote his first novel (*Immaturity*) but failed to find a publisher for it. This and the other four novels which reached completion at yearly intervals were products of conscientious industry: 'I bought supplies of white paper, demy size, by sixpennorths at a time; folded it in quarto; and condemned myself to fill five pages of it a day, rain or shine, dull or inspired. I had so much of the schoolboy and the clerk still in me that if my five pages ended in the middle of a sentence I did not

[1] Preface (1921) to *Immaturity*, p. xxxiv. Page references throughout are to the Standard Edition of Shaw's works, as published by Constable.

[2] When giving these figures Shaw overlooked eighteen guineas paid to him by Vandeleur Lee for eighteen articles in *The Hornet* from 29 November 1876 to 28 March 1877. The articles (music criticisms) were printed as by Lee. In making no public mention of them Shaw may have wished not to reveal Lee's subterfuge. The receipted account in Shaw's handwriting is reproduced in facsimile by O'Donovan, op. cit.

finish it until next day.'[1] The fifth novel, *An Unsocial Socialist*, was the first to get into print, as a serial in a periodical named *To-day*, in 1884; the fourth, *Cashel Byron's Profession*, came out in the same paper in 1885–6; the second, *The Irrational Knot*, ran serially in 1885–7 and the third, *Love Among the Artists*, in 1887-8—both in *Our Corner*, a magazine controlled by Mrs Annie Besant, whom Shaw afterwards converted to Fabian Socialism, and who was in later years a prominent theosophist and leader in the political campaign for Indian independence. It is probable that none of these novels would have been reissued in after years but for their author's later eminence in other fields. Yet they still have interest for those patient enough to read them, and the later Shaw found in *The Irrational Knot* (which on literary grounds he dismissed as a jejune exploit) a closeness to the Ibsenite attitude years before Ibsen's writings became known to him.[2] This is a point of special importance, since Bernard Shaw is often regarded as a disciple of Ibsen whose work would have been altogether different in character, or might not have existed at all, if Ibsen had not led the way. In *The Irrational Knot*, however, as he says, 'the morality is original and not ready-made . . . the revolt of the Life Force against ready-made morality in the nineteenth century was not the work of a Norwegian microbe, but would have worked itself into expression in English literature had Norway never existed'.[3]

When the last of the novels, *An Unsocial Socialist*, was written in 1883, five unpublished manuscripts were the only visible product of Shaw's first seven years in London. It was clear that the novel was an unsuitable literary medium for him, and one in which the utmost perseverance and painstaking industry would bring him little reward. The slow tread of narrative and the thick verbal substance from which novels must be hewn were hampering to his arrowlike mind,

[1] Preface (1921) to *Immaturity*, p. xxxvii.

[2] Preface (1905) to *The Irrational Knot*.

[3] Nevertheless in the Preface to *Three Unpleasant Plays* (*Plays Pleasant and Unpleasant*, Vol. I, 1898) he had written that the New Drama 'would never have come into existence but for the plays of Ibsen'.

which shot ahead while a novelist's only plodded. Since a speaker is able to cover in an hour what might occupy a novelist for a whole week, the spoken rather than the written word was surely Bernard Shaw's foreordained medium. He had to learn to speak before he could succeed as an author; and it is no doubt symptomatic of his impatience with the tedious labour of adding written word to written word that he learned shorthand and used it thereafter for most of his manuscripts. The drama is the literary medium for speech, and to the drama Shaw was accordingly led by his daemon; but the progression was slow, and for years he must himself have been totally unaware of what lay before him. His apprenticeship was to politics and economics, not to the theatre; to the platform, not to the stage. In that seemingly roundabout route to the fulfilment of his destiny, however, lay also the secret of his unique success.

The playwright's art consists particularly in the ability to provide actors with *speakable* words and the audience with words that are immediately intelligible. A novelist need only provide *readable* words. His task is easier than the playwright's in two respects: a reader's eye can cope with phrases that would require to be composed more euphoniously if they were intended to be spoken; and a reader can also ponder and absorb at his own mental pace, however slow, such complexities of thought and meaning as may be embedded in a novelist's prose. There are practised playwrights who have never mastered the art of the spoken word; their dialogue does not come naturally from a speaker's mouth. Dialogue of that sort can only be used to convey elementary thoughts and ideas, for the ears of the audience are not helped to ease the way to mental apprehension. Because of such verbal ineptitude, even playwrights of repute may compose plays which are deplorably meagre in content. The prime facts about Shaw's plays are that his words are always easy on the actors' tongues, and therefore on the listeners' ears also; and that their content is rich and ample and intellectually rewarding. His ideas are absorbed even by unready hearers. There is, of course, no way of calculating the number of those who have been influenced by Shaw against their will, but his skill was such that by persuasive insinuation his words creep into ears and go into minds that may wish to close against them, and germinate where they would otherwise remain sterile.

It has been necessary to wrest from their proper chronological place in Shaw's life-story these observations upon an important aspect of his plays, in order to indicate the permanent importance of his early years in London, years which were apparently so unfruitful for literature. They were in truth the seed-time preparatory to a harvest such as British drama had not known in the three centuries since Shakespear died in 1616.

III

In 1879 Shaw was taken by a friend to a debate held by the Zetetical Society,[1] a body which met regularly in London to discuss public affairs in the light of the doctrine enunciated in John Stuart Mill's *Essay on Liberty* (1859). During that debate Shaw spoke for the first time in public and was so nervous, forgetting his main points, that he determined to seek thenceforward every opportunity for addressing audiences, and so turn himself into a lucid and effective public speaker. At that time he was shy and awkward and self-conscious. Even when he went to visit friends in private he was so unsure of himself that he would sometimes walk up and down the street for a long while before he could bring himself to knock at the door. So also, he records, he suffered agonies that no one suspected while carrying out his resolution to become an orator. He spoke in debates, gave lectures, harangued meetings at street-corners and in the parks, until he became acknowledged as one of the foremost public speakers, unsurpassed for clarity, cogency, assurance, and sanity. He became known

[1] *zetetic*, proceeding by inquiry.

everywhere as 'G.B.S.'; though G.B.S., he insisted, was a consciously self-created character, created as an actor creates a role in the theatre, and created as a figure to hide the natural Shaw whose instinctive reserve was a severe disability. In creating the part of G.B.S. he created it with scrupulous solidity and in full detail: it became a three-dimensional personality, completely alive in every sense. Exercising the function of Pygmalion, he made not a Galatea but another Pygmalion—an improved model. The self-distrusting young man of twenty-three who first spoke to the Zetetical Society in 1879 became the world-famous Bernard Shaw who filled the Metropolitan Opera House in New York in 1933, and whose career as 'a platform artist' lasted until 1941, when he retired from public speaking at the age of eighty-three; sixty years of oratory in which sense and sound were well balanced. Of his platform technique he wrote: '. . . to be intelligible in public the speaker must relearn the alphabet with every consonant separately and explosively articulated, and foreign vowels distinguished from British diphthongs, Accordingly I practise the alphabet as a singer practises scales. . . .'[1]

So much for the sound. What of the sense?

In 1884 Shaw went one evening to a meeting in the Memorial Hall in Farringdon Street, London, at which Henry George, 'American apostle of Land Nationalization and Single Tax' and author of *Progress and Poverty*, was the speaker. Shaw's conversion to Socialism took place on that evening. In a Nonconformist building where others had 'found religion' of a different kind, he found his own life-religion through economics. Soon afterwards he read Karl Marx for the first time (in French; no English translation had then been made) and found in Marxian economics a reinforcement of his lately acquired conversion to Henry-Georgian economics. After that, Shaw consistently proclaimed himself a Socialist; but his socialism was always secondary to his inborn individualism. Never conformable

[1] 'How I Became a Public Speaker': *Sixteen Self Sketches*, p. 64.

to a party doctrine, he lived to hear himself abused by Communists as a Fascist and by Fascists as a Communist, and by party men of all colours as an advocate of whatever other -ism they most hated. Under the rule of any kind of persecuting dogmatism he would have been liable to martyrdom. He was the arch-independent of his time, and to that must be attributed his attraction to Joan of Arc and his play *Saint Joan*—in which, characteristically, he also sets out a powerful case *against* as well as *for* nonconformity. These inconsistencies, as many have taken them to be, this apparent double and contrarious vision, he himself credited to his rare possession of normal sight. He tells in the Preface to his first book of plays[1] of how he visited an ophthalmic surgeon who 'tested my eyesight one evening, and informed me that it was quite uninteresting to him because it was normal. . . . I was an exceptional and highly fortunate person optically, normal sight conferring the power of seeing things accurately, and being enjoyed by only about ten per cent of the population. . . . I immediately perceived the explanation of my want of success in fiction. My mind's eye, like my body's was "normal": it saw things differently from other people's eyes, and saw them better.'[2]

It is not at all necessary to agree with Shaw's persuasion that mentally as well as physically he saw things better than other people saw them, in order to recognize how serviceable was this ability to see differently, whether the difference of vision tends towards accuracy or towards aberration. It was as an irritant, compelling the repeated questioning and re-examination of passively accepted current standards of value, that he was important. Very few even among his ardent disciples accepted his gospel wholly or without question. To do so would have been a traitorous negation of Shaw's gospel, for its main tenet is that nothing should be approved by the adult mind until its validity has been

[1] Preface to *Three Unpleasant Plays* (*Plays Pleasant and Unpleasant*, Vol. I, 1898).

[2] ibid., p. vi.

established in experience. This is the logical extension of the dialectical technique of Socrates: the empirical test 'Does it work?' following the metaphysical inquiry 'Is it true?'; the conviction that such basic questions as 'Is religious faith a duty?', 'Is marriage sacred?', 'Is science immune from superstition?', 'Is parliamentary democracy real democracy?' cannot be answered without a fair and full weighing of the consequences of these things in history past and present. So, to Shaw, Socialism was neither an immutable dogma nor a sentimental creed: 'Socialism to me has always meant, not a principle, but certain definite economic measures which I wish to see taken.'[1] What those measures are was set out by him in exhaustive detail in *The Intelligent Woman's Guide to Socialism and Capitalism* (1928) and *Everybody's Political What's What* (1943).

Because it was the economics of Socialism and not its heroics that converted him in 1884, he supported the Fabian Society, which was founded in that year. He joined the Fabians without delay and addressed himself to the prosecution of their aims, which were mainly (after their first militant phase): to frame a working parliamentary programme for a British Socialist government when such a government should be elected; to attract to Socialism, by education and studied methods of moderation, types and classes of people who would not countenance extremism. There were rival socialist organizations in existence already, committed to anarchism or other forms of direct action; but the Fabian Society outlived them and effectively propagated its policy.

Shaw also persuaded Sidney Webb, whom he first met at the Zetetical Society in 1879, to join the infant Fabian Society, and together they set to work to make Socialism 'constitutional, respectable, and practical'. They remained close friends and colleagues until Webb died nearly seventy years later (in 1947, aged eighty-eight). In Shaw's opinion Webb was 'the ablest man in England', and he said that

[1] 'The Impossibilities of Anarchism' (1893): *Essays in Fabian Socialism*, (1932).

from the time they became acquainted he was no longer 'a futile Shaw but a committee of Webb and Shaw'.[1] Webb and his wife (*née* Beatrice Potter) were a unique pair of single-minded, whole-hearted, indefatigable investigators and researchers whose massive publications on the Poor Law, on Local Government, and on other economic and political subjects are indispensable documents for legislators, administrators, and scholars. Their work was exclusively for human betterment, yet a common impression developed outside their personal circle that they were themselves deficient in the warmer qualities of humanity; that they saw men and women as statistics walking. This was, in some degree at least, a false impression. Nevertheless they were interpreted by many as types of almost disembodied intelligence, insusceptible to the hopes and fears and passions which beset most of mankind. So, although their self-abnegating work was a unique feat of mental application, as collectors of facts and figures they failed to quicken the public imagination.[2] It remained for Shaw himself to perform this invaluable service, and in so far as he and Webb constituted a committee in any sense, it was Shaw who rendered palatable to the national audience the findings of that committee of two, humanizing and much enlivening and, it may well be, immortalizing Webb as well as himself in this act of transmission.

IV

The first phase of Bernard Shaw's career closed in 1876 with his abandonment of office employment and his removal

[1] 'Fruitful Friendships': *Sixteen Self Sketches*, p. 65.

[2] Certain observations in Beatrice Webb's published diaries show that while she had a theoretical concern for the welfare of people as a mass, she was often arrogantly contemptuous of individuals. In *The New Machiavelli* (1911) H. G. Wells, who had been a dissident Fabian, portrayed the Webbs satirically as Oscar and Altiora Bailey, saying of Oscar that he had a mind 'as orderly as a museum' and of Altiora that 'she saw men as samples moving'.

to London. His second phase can be said to have ended with 1884, by which time he had become a public speaker, a Fabian, a writer with five inauspicious novels behind him, a vegetarian and sort of atheist as the result of reading Shelley. Among the consequences of an attack of smallpox in 1881 were an auburn beard which he never afterwards shaved and a distinctive Mephistophelian moustache. They seemed a challenge flung out to defenders of the old order against which Shaw was crusading; while the snowy beard of his age fitted well the patriarchal role assigned to him when, though still remaining the challenger and fighter, he became an established institution in the intellectual landscape of the nineteen-twenties to forties. Modern Britain does not martyrize its rebels; it tolerates them with more or less impatience while they are young; admires them, enjoys them, even canonizes them without benefit of Church, when they grow old. In his own unofficial canonization Shaw's beard was of no small importance. It enabled him to assume the appearance of a saint without entirely shedding that of Mephistopheles. His vegetarianism (which, he claimed, would entitle his funeral to be followed by 'herds of oxen, sheep, swine, flocks of poultry, and a small travelling aquarium of live fish, all wearing white scarves') may have contributed to his longevity; it was certainly often a cause of humour in others. The most frequently repeated of the vegetarian quips, which became current in several versions, came from the actress Mrs Patrick Campbell (the original Eliza Doolittle in Shaw's *Pygmalion*) who, during rehearsals of the play, was said to have exclaimed, 'One of these days Shaw will eat a beef steak, and then God help all women!'[1]

His formal career as a journalist began in 1885 when William Archer, dramatic critic and translator of Ibsen into English, introduced him as a book reviewer to *The Pall Mall Gazette*, and in the next year to *The World* as art critic.

[1] See Hesketh Pearson, *Bernard Shaw: His Life and Personality* (1942), p. 298, for the authentic version.

He also began his first play, *Widowers' Houses*, in 1885, basing it on plot-material supplied by Archer. Shaw declared that he used up Archer's 'well made' plot in a few sentences, whereupon Archer retired from the collaboration and the unfinished play was abandoned for seven years. The art criticisms in *The World* (they have not been reprinted in book form) continued until 1889, a year after Shaw had been found too provocative as a political writer for *The Star*, a London evening newspaper started in 1888. *The Star* retained him, however, as music critic. The articles he contributed from 14 May 1888 to 16 May 1890 were reissued (1937) in the volume entitled *London Music in 1888–9 as heard by Corno di Bassetto (later known as Bernard Shaw)*. Until Shaw began, it had been usual for newspaper criticism of the arts to be anonymous, but he thought impersonal criticism worthless and adopted a pen name (his own was not then familiar to the reading public). 'I had to invent a fantastic personality with something like a foreign title', he said, and chose Corno di Bassetto (basset horn, in English), an instrument now displaced in the orchestra by the bass clarinet. When he took this pseudonym Shaw was unaware that the basset horn has a peculiar 'watery melancholy' and a 'total absence of any richness or passion in its tone'. 'If I had ever heard a note of it in 1888 I should not have selected it for a character which I intended to be sparkling.'

There was no watery melancholy, no want of passion, in the articles. Fifty years afterwards, when his wife urged that they should be reissued, their author found them occasionally vulgar and tending towards ribaldry. But, however noisily they struck the Shavian chord, the genuine accent and tone later to become famous were already there. He left *The Star* in order to do music criticism for *The World* (his articles there were reprinted in three volumes, 1931, as *Music in London* 1890–4), resigning when Edmund Yates, the editor, died. Then in 1895 he was appointed dramatic critic to *The Saturday Review* by Frank Harris, under whose editorship that weekly journal provided for several years one of the most brilliant and substantial chapters in the history of British journalism. Week by week from 5 January 1895 until 14 May 1898 Shaw, above the signature G.B.S., wrote what became in total the most remarkable series of articles that any writer has produced on plays and players in the London theatre.

Something of the background to British theatrical activity at that period needs to be shown in connection with these *Saturday Review* articles (reprinted in three volumes, 1931, as *Our Theatres in the Nineties*).

Goldsmith's *She Stoops to Conquer* was first performed in 1773, Sheridan's *The Rivals* in 1775 and *The School for Scandal* in 1777. From then until T. W. Robertson's *Caste* was performed in 1867 no new British play of social interest and literary merit had appeared on the stage. There had been a succession of great actors and actresses, but their talents were exercised mainly in revivals (varying in merit) of works by Shakespear and other classic dramatists. Shelley, Browning, and Tennyson wrote a few plays, but did not possess enough practical knowledge of the theatre to enable them to employ poetry rightly for the stage. Drudging adapters and translators rushed out dramatized versions of popular novels by Scott and Dickens and turned into careless English dozens of foreign plays, mostly paltry bowdlerized Parisian popular successes. A few British playwrights supplied spectacular sensational melodramas with effective acting parts for leading actors. In short, the drama had ceased to be a branch of British literature, as it was in the sixteenth century with the plays of Shakespear, Marlowe, and others; in the seventeenth century with Ben Jonson, Congreve, and Wycherley; in the eighteenth with Goldsmith and Sheridan. Acting had entirely lost contact with life and was no mirror held up to nature; the stage had become the home of falsity and extravagant impossibility; the word 'theatrical' was taken into common use to denote whatever was unreal and unlifelike. Attempts were made in the earlier part of the nineteenth century to produce Shakespear's plays with correct period costumes and scenery, but throughout the century little respect was paid to the presentation of an accurate text or to the proper speaking of his poetry.

The steps taken by T. W. Robertson in the direction of a new type of naturalistic play now seem only short and timid, but in the circumstances of the eighteen-sixties they were important and on the right road. *Caste* can still be seen and read with attention and respect after a century. It brought back to the stage the breath of contemporary life and showed average people behaving more or less in an average way and in average circumstances. Following Robertson came A. W. Pinero (himself at first an actor, in conscious preparation for the career of dramatist which he planned to adopt) and Henry Arthur Jones. Both were established playwrights when Shaw started as dramatic critic, and both had brought to the stage a further breath of naturalism. Though in some respects they were more artificial than Robertson, they set a higher literary standard. Robertson belonged to the stage, and to the stage alone. Jones and Pinero could claim to belong also to literature, if only to its fringes.[1] Both could tell absorbing stories in stage dialogue, and some of their plays can still be read with pleasure. Both were in some measure—though reluctantly—influenced by one greater than themselves, the Norwegian poet and dramatist Henrik Ibsen, whose poetic dramas *Brand* (1865) and *Peer Gynt* (1867) preceded his social problem plays in prose, *A Doll's House* (1878–9) and its successors, which were to shake the British theatre and (at length) British prejudice and complacency. *A Doll's House* did not reach the London stage until 1889.

In 1891 Bernard Shaw wrote the first book in English on Ibsen, *The Quintessence of Ibsenism* (revised and enlarged in 1913, and included in *Major Critical Essays*, 1930). Pinero's *The Second Mrs Tanqueray* was produced in London in 1893,

[1] Pinero's *Trelawny of the 'Wells'* (1899) was taken successfully into the repertory of the National Theatre some half century later. The character Tom Wrench is modelled on T. W. Robertson.

and the fact that the play represented a misconception of Ibsen's aims and was an unconscious travesty of them, does not hide that Ibsenism was seeping into the minds of even those British dramatists who had no sympathy with Ibsen. Pinero's fundamental weakness lay in his inability or unwillingness to take a genuine social or other human problem as the core of a play. He invented artificial stage plots and sought to give them a serious interest which the shoddy material could not sustain. He was accepted by British theatregoers as an 'advanced' dramatist, as 'a man of new ideas', but he was no more than a protective buffer which, for a while, absorbed and nullified the crashing impact of Norwegian realism. Shaw refused to accept Pinero as a serious dramatist. He found embryonic merits in *The Second Mrs Tanqueray*, but declared that 'the moment the point is reached at which the comparatively common gift of "an eye for a character" has to be supplemented by the higher dramatic gift of sympathy with character—of the power of seeing the world from the point of view of others instead of merely describing or judging them from one's own point of view in terms of the conventional systems of morals, Mr Pinero breaks down'.[1] He was kinder to his friend Henry Arthur Jones, pleading that Jones's attack on lower middle-class hypocrisy was 'courageous, uncompromising, made with sharp weapons, and left without the slightest attempt to run away at the end'.[2]

Neither Pinero nor Jones now seems a major figure in the development of the modern British theatre. Since Pinero never handled a genuine social or moral problem, the few of his plays that have survived do so as good entertainment, without further pretensions. Jones did attempt a serious criticism of contemporary standards, yet when his plays are now re-read they seem to fail at the very point where Shaw thought they succeeded. Jones did not face up boldly

[1] *The Saturday Review*, 23 February 1895 (*Our Theatres in the Nineties*, I, pp. 46-47).

[2] 18 May 1895 (op. cit., I, 127).

to the problems he posed in his plays, and in their final scenes he often fell back upon what was, at bottom, a second-hand and stale morality. Shaw, it must be remembered, was crusading for Ibsen and was therefore disposed to welcome any genuine sign of an Ibsenite approach in British drama. If he overpraised Jones it was because Jones raised hopes and expectations which it could not then be foreseen that his later works would disappoint. He fell short of Ibsen's unique achievement, which was, as Shaw said, to proffer a morality which was original all through.[1] 'In the theatre of Ibsen we are not flattered spectators killing an idle hour with an ingenious and amusing entertainment: we are "guilty creatures sitting at a play".'[2]

Throughout his *Saturday Review* period Shaw's Ibsen campaign put him at variance with the outstanding London actor-managers, particularly with Henry Irving—then the most powerful personality on the English stage—who had the greatest contemporary English actress, Ellen Terry, as his leading lady for many years at the Lyceum Theatre. Shaw held that the unique talents of these two should have been given to the service of the new drama, instead of being confined to Shakespearian revivals, romantic historical plays, and melodrama. The progress of the struggle against Irving can be followed in the remarkable series of letters which passed (1892–1922; but they were few and less important after December 1900) between Shaw and Ellen Terry.[3] The struggle generated a delusion which is still prevalent that Shaw was an anti-Shakespearian and that he claimed to be greater than Shakespear. His real case was that ill service had been done to Shakespear by modern performances, Irving's among them, in which stress was laid not on the dramatic poetry but on 'a gorgeous stage ritualism superimposed on reckless mutilations of his text',[4] to the injury of the best

[1] *The Irrational Knot*. Postscript to Preface (1905), p. xvii.
[2] *Major Critical Essays*, p.146.
[3] Published in 1931 as *Ellen Terry and Bernard Shaw: A Correspondence*, with a valuable Preface by Shaw.
[4] Preface (1900) to *Three Plays for Puritans*, p. xi.

qualities in Shakespear, 'unsurpassed as poet, storyteller, character draughtsman, humorist, and rhetorician'.[1] For himself Shaw claimed no more than that a modern author could legitimately profess to have something to say that was important to modern people, something that Shakespear could not possibly have said in his century—even as Shakespear had been able to present Achilles and Ajax in a light not available to Homer. Shaw's objection was to what he called 'bardolatry', the unintelligent worship of Shakespear and the pretence that Shakespear had not left unsaid anything that it was vital to say in the changed circumstances and needs of the nineteenth–twentieth century.

Now that the heat of old controversies has cooled, Shaw's dramatic criticisms can be read with calm attention to their analytical and literary merits. Many of the plays examined in them are long since forgotten, yet what Shaw had to say even about the least of them is still full of interest. He wrote as a man with a well stored mind and a ready gift of expression upon which he could draw for substance and vivacity, for analogy and light. In a week of dull plays and indifferent acting he could always turn to consider the theatre of his own mind, in which some fascinating fragment of the drama of life was always on-stage.

The enlargement of Corno di Bassetto into G.B.S. was the pre-natal stage of Bernard Shaw the dramatist. A foot injury and breakdown from overwork led to his retirement from *The Saturday Review* in 1898. In the last of his weekly contributions he wrote: 'For ten years past, with an unprecedented pertinacity and obstination, I have been dinning into the public head that I am an extraordinarily witty, brilliant, and clever man. That is now part of the public opinion of England; and no power in heaven or on earth will ever change it. I may dodder and dote; I may potboil and platitudinize; I may become the butt and chopping-block of all bright, original spirits of the rising generation;

[1] Preface to *Three Unpleasant Plays* (*Plays Pleasant and Unpleasant*, Vol. I, 1898), p. xix.

but my reputation shall not suffer: it is built up fast and solid, like Shakespear's, on an impregnable basis of dogmatic reiteration.' More than half a century later it could be seen that, by whatever means Shaw's reputation was built, it was certainly built up fast and solid.

V

In 1886 the Shelley Society arranged in London a private performance of Shelley's poetic tragedy *The Cenci*, which the censor had prohibited from stage production in public. It was played before an invited audience, the general public was excluded, and no admission money was taken at the doors.[1] This was an important occasion in the history of the modern British theatre, since it meant that for the first time a way had been found to circumvent the censor's ban on plays of social and literary value which did not conform with current conventional opinion. Opponents of the censorship complained that plays in which serious problems were seriously discussed were refused a licence by the censor, whereas frivolous plays dabbling in sex received official approval, however debasing they might be to public taste and morality.

A year later (1887), André Antoine, an amateur actor, founded Le Théâtre Libre in Paris for the production of new plays which failed to attract the commercial theatre managers. Antoine's example, and the demonstration by the Shelley Society that the British censor's authority could not be extended to hamper 'private' performances, moved J. T. Grein, a young naturalized Englishman of Dutch birth who was writing dramatic criticism in London, to found the Independent Theatre Society in 1891. The first play to be performed (on 13 March in that year) was William Archer's

[1] This practice was more or less loosely followed until the Theatres Act 1968 abolished stage censorship after repeated campaigns against it. See for example Shaw's 'Preface on the Censorship' to *The Shewing-up of Blanco Posnet*.

translation of Ibsen's *Ghosts*. Then Bernard Shaw turned back to the uncompleted 1885 script of his own *Widowers' Houses*. He completed it in 1892, Grein having promised in advance to put it on the stage, though he knew nothing about it except that the third act was still to be written. So the first Shaw play had its first performance under the auspices of the Independent Theatre Society at the Royalty Theatre in London on 9 December 1892. Though it was discussed in the newspapers for a fortnight, the hope that it might then be taken up by some commercial manager for public production went unfulfilled, and it was not seen again for thirty years. In a belated revival of this play in 1949 (at the Arts Theatre, London) a new generation found it still absorbing in subject, still amusing and witty, and still interesting in characterization since it sketches in outline certain types which were developed in Shaw's later plays.[1] The word 'types', however, must in this application be qualified and limited. While it is true that Shaw's characters are often, in essence, personified ideas or attitudes, they are always more than puppets, more than mouthpieces for the author. They have a life of their own. This has often been disputed,[2] but it cannot be gainsaid by any who have come to close quarters with them while performing in Shaw's plays and have found that his characters have more to give to the actors than the actors can give to them. No play lives by ideas alone, however important its ideas may be at the moment it is written. The ideas in *Widowers' Houses* are no longer fresh or startling. The problem of slum property still exists, but it is a different problem nowadays from what it was in 1892; and if the play had been only an exposure of 'middle-class respectability and younger son gentility fattening on the poverty of the slums as flies fatten on filth'[3] it would by now have become an historical relic, a social

[1] Compare, for example, Lickcheese in *Widowers' Houses* with Burgess in *Candida* and Alfred Doolittle in *Pygmalion*.

[2] It continued to be disputed at intervals by imperceptive journalists and academics lacking theatre sense.

[3] Preface to *Widowers' Houses*, p. xxii.

tract in dramatic form interesting to students but scarcely entertaining to a theatre audience. We have to look to other factors to account for its survival as a stage play.

The men in *Widowers' Houses* are common self-seekers, and the heroine a fury who half-strangles her maid in a fit of temper; but Shaw from the beginning grasped the fact that every human being, whether scoundrel or saint, has a point of view which makes it possible for him to justify himself to himself—and at need, he hopes, to others also. The scoundrel is a man of principle in his own eyes, and society cannot go far towards uprooting scoundrelism until it sees the scoundrel as he sees himself. This is what Shaw set out to do for society, by an act of the imagination: not simply to preach against and vilify scoundrels, not simply to praise and magnify non-scoundrels, but to create scoundrels as well as non-scoundrels three-dimensionally, in the round, so that they live and move and have their being in the sight and sound of the audience, exposing themselves in the penetrating light of their own self-justification.

In a passage quoted above (page 26) Shaw speaks of 'the power of seeing the world from the point of view of others instead of merely describing or judging them from one's own point of view in terms of the conventional systems of morals'. That is the power Pinero lacked. It is the power with which Shaw was fully equipped. His characters live on the stage as themselves; they present their own case: it is the business and the pleasure of the audience, not the duty of the dramatist, to give a verdict after the evidence on both sides has been heard.

One of the curiosities of popular criticism of Shaw is the complaint, on the one hand, that his characters are merely mouthpieces for his own ideas—that they preach openly or by implication Shaw's own gospel; and, on the other hand, that Shaw was a purely destructive critic with no gospel to offer. The first complaint cannot be upheld if the sayings of Shaw's characters are fairly weighed and balanced: for example (from many that could be cited), who is Shaw's mouthpiece in *Saint Joan*—Joan herself? or Warwick? or Cauchon? or the Inquisitor? Each presents a valid case from opposing angles. In *The Apple Cart*, is it King Magnus or the Prime Minister that is Shaw's mouthpiece? Each presents his own case, and the two are irreconcilable. The second complaint, that Shaw was nothing but a destructive critic, can only be interpreted as an unflattering reflection upon adult mentality. Shaw assumed that audiences are capable of drawing a constructive conclusion from the presentation of abundant evidence. If this assumption is unwarranted it must appear that Man is incapable of choosing between good and evil and that his case is hopeless, a desolating view to which Shaw never subscribed; though he frequently gave warning that, unless we learn how to live and put our world-house in order, the Life Force (Shaw's synonym for Nature, or Providence, or whatever name be given to the driving power of the universe) will destroy Man and replace him by some superior creature—the Superman—conformable to its will, as the mammoths were destroyed and superseded by Man. In Act III of *Man and Superman* Don Juan says: 'Things immeasurably greater than Man in every respect but brain have existed and perished. The megatherium, the ichthyosaurus have paced the earth with seven-league steps and hidden the day with their cloud vast wings. Where are they now? Fossils in museums. . . . These things lived and wanted to live; but for lack of brains they did not know how to carry out their purpose, and so destroyed themselves. . . .' When the Devil replies that Man too is destroying himself by wonderful inventions which promote the art of death and negate the art of living, Don Juan claims that Man *will* save himself if he can be persuaded that he is fighting for a mighty idea: 'This creature Man, who in his own selfish affairs is a coward to the backbone, will fight for an idea like a hero . . . if you can show a man a piece of what he now calls God's work to do, and what he will later on call by many new names, you can make him entirely reckless of the consequences to him personally.' Salvation was always, for Bernard Shaw, the experience of being seized by a mighty purpose: what Tanner in Act I of *Man and Superman* calls 'moral passion', the birth of which took control of all his common passions and organized them into 'an army of purposes and principles. My soul was born of the moral passion.'

Moral passion is the power unit—the virtue—in all the 'good' characters in Shaw's plays, and the virtue lives in its own right and is its own reward. In *The Devil's Disciple* Dick Dudgeon lets himself be arrested as a rebel in mistake for another man, although he knows that he is almost certain to be condemned and hanged. He rebuts the suggestion that he imperilled himself because he was in love with the other man's wife and wished to save the husband for her sake. He was moved not by romantic love, not by any romantic notion of self-sacrifice, but by some deep-seated impelling virtue which he cannot truly comprehend. In *Major Barbara* Barbara (of the Salvation Army) cries: 'I have got rid of the bribe of heaven. Let God's work be done for its own sake: the work he had to create us to do because it cannot be done except by living men and women.' In *The Shewing-up of Blanco Posnet* it is the apparently 'bad' man, the horse thief, who is seized by the transforming moral passion which compels him to give up to a woman with a sick child the stolen horse which would have carried him to safety. He is puzzled by the sudden inner compulsion to perform a virtuous act, 'but I lost the rotten feel all the same'. When he is told that it was the Lord speaking to his soul, he scoffs; yet he goes on to say in a sudden blaze of illumination: '. . . You bet He didn't make us for nothing; and He wouldn't have made us at all if He could have done His work without us. By Gum, that must be what we're for! . . . He made me because He had a job for me. He let me run loose till the job was ready; and then I had to come along and do it, hanging or no hanging. . . . Anyhow, I got the rotten feel off me for a minute of my life; and I'll go through fire to get it off me again. . . .'

Although Shaw was repeatedly upbraided by Christian people as a scoffer at sacred things, in matters of conduct and true virtue there is little if any ground for their complaining against him. His main point of dissent from Christian belief is seen in his statement that 'I detest the doctrine of the Atonement, holding that ladies and gentlemen cannot as such possibly allow anyone else to expiate their sins by suffering a cruel death.'[1] His positive denomination for himself was 'Creative Evolutionist', but he recognized that the general acceptance of belief in Creative Evolution can come only as a stage in the evolutionary process and that to attempt to convert the unready would be disastrous and merely turn them into savages 'with no scruples, no personal god (the only sort of God they could believe in), and no fear of hell to restrain them',[2] a forecast substantiated in modern political dogmas and in the widespread relapse into barbarism.

Shaw's belief in the Life Force and in Creative Evolution stands as the main trunk of his work, formed by *Man and Superman* and *Back to Methuselah*. His other plays are the branches of the tree. In these he discusses problems of marriage (*The Philanderer; Candida; Getting Married; Misalliance*), of family life (*You Never Can Tell; Fanny's First Play*), of sexual prostitution and its economic roots (*Mrs Warren's Profession*), of politics and statecraft (*John Bull's Other Island; Heartbreak House; The Apple Cart; Too True to be Good; On the Rocks*), of religion (*Androcles and the Lion; Saint Joan*). None of the plays is confined to the discussion of problems, however.

Ibsen's opposition to the romantic attitude first attracted Shaw to the Norwegian dramatist's work, and Shaw's own early plays are Ibsenite in their striving to gain assent to such realities as that war is not romantic (*Arms and the Man*); that marriage has a stern biological purpose—at the disposition of the Life Force—to which romantic love is no more

[1] 'What is My Religious Faith?': *Sixteen Self Sketches*, p. 73.
[2] ibid., p. 79.

than an enticing prelude; and that self-sacrifice may be nothing better than a cloak for the sacrifice of others to one's own self-will, self-indulgence, possessiveness, or spiritual pride. But it must be said again that Shaw as a dramatist holds the balance fairly between his own views and those of his opponents. What his own views were has been made known in the famous Prefaces (which are not always closely relevant to the plays they precede) and through his other non-dramatic writings.

The Preface to *Man and Superman* announced his own convictions about the Life Force. In the play itself the utterances of John Tanner-Don Juan (the two characters are really one and the same) are eloquently and ably disputed in Act III by the Devil, and anyone who so chooses may find the Devil more persuasive than his opponent. In the *Back to Methuselah* Preface Shaw set out his philosophy (or religion) of Creative Evolution. The play itself—which is in five parts, each forming a separable play—envisages the term of individual human life extended to centuries instead of remaining at a few decades as now. Shaw doubts 'whether the human animal, as he exists at present, is capable of solving the social problems raised by his own aggregation, or, as he calls it, his civilization'.[1] Whatever wisdom the human being does acquire is lost at his all-too-early death, and Shaw postulates Creative Evolution as the only possible means of remedying the twentieth-century plight of man and his civilization. He held that Darwin's Natural Selection is not Evolution; that it is external, accidental, and mechanistic; that man's conscious desire and will have no place in it. Creative Evolution substitutes for Darwinism the idea (Shaw called it a simple fact) that the human 'will to do anything can and does, at a certain pitch of intensity set up by a conviction of its necessity, create and organize new tissue to do it with'.[2] Only if life be lengthened, by the deliberate opera-

[1] Preface to *Back to Methuselah*, p. x.
[2] ibid., p. xvi.

tion of Man's will, can Man realize his potentialities. Only then will mankind discover an adequate motive for the abolition of war and disease and such other preventable ills as now frustrate the Life Force.

In the final speech of *Back to Methuselah* Lilith's concluding lines run: '. . . Of Life only is there no end; and though of its million starry mansions many are empty and many still unbuilt, and though its vast domain is yet unbearably desert, my seed shall one day fill it and master its matter to its uttermost confines. And for what may be beyond, the eyesight of Lilith is too short. It is enough that there is a beyond.'

VI

It was for some half-century the settled opinion of the British that Bernard Shaw was a revolutionary; but few had any clear notion of what it was that he revolutionized. His influence on contemporary social and political thought was certainly important, though it is impossible to assess its extent or its depth, for it has merged pervasively into the intellectual atmosphere of the twentieth century and no one could measure Shaw's own contribution to the changes of outlook which have come about in this age of bewilderingly accelerated change. Here, in summary, our view must be limited to the revolution effected by his plays (*a*) on the stage and (*b*) in print.

Literature students in search of definitions meet, soon or late, the formula *Drama is conflict*. A great deal of critical disapproval of Shaw's plays was based upon the supposition that they lack this primary element of conflict. If conflict in drama necessarily implies a clash involving either violent physical action or intense emotional disturbance, then conflict in that sense is lacking in the Shavian drama. It is, however, intentionally lacking, and its place is taken by mental action, which to Shaw was far more exciting. For the conflict of passion Shaw substituted the conflict of

thought and belief; or, rather, he brought moral passion on to the stage to break the long monopoly of physical and sensual passion. His is the drama of the thinking man, challenging the drama of the lusting man. The true revolution which must be ascribed to him is the transference of conflict in modern drama from the physical to the mental plane. Discussion is the root of all Shaw's plays, and audiences were by reluctant degrees compelled by his intense conviction and cajoled by his flashing wit and buoyant humour to acknowledge that mental conflict—the clash of competing ideas and of opposing standards of human values—can provide highly acceptable, absorbing, and entertaining dramatic material. This revolution was, as most revolutions are, a return and a revival. In all great drama, and especially in that of classical Greece and Elizabethan England, the collision of ideas is of paramount importance. In Shaw's plays, however, there is no recourse to the catastrophic violence which provided the inevitable climax in poetic tragedy. Shaw grew up and matured in a period when argument appeared likely to become man's master-weapon, and when no Briton could have believed that by the middle of the twentieth century the tragic dilemma of Antigone would have come to seem more immediate than the domestic dilemma of Candida.

When Bernard Shaw adopted the theatre as his forum he was aware of its limitations for his purpose. It certainly permitted him to reach a larger audience than had heard him as a platform orator indoors and out of doors; yet even so, as he was to point out a few years later in the Preface to *Unpleasant Plays*, the English had lost the theatregoing habit. At that time, too, it was not the more thoughtful nor the socially conscientious who frequented the theatre. Consequently, with the intention of multiplying his audience, Shaw started to publish his plays in printed form. But the non-playgoing public was also a non-playreading public. Was this the fault of the public? Or was it because plays were published in a style which discouraged potential readers? Shaw thought that the fault lay with the printed plays more than with the public. So, having already launched one revolution in regard to plays on the stage, he followed it with a revolution in regard to plays in print.

Until then, playwrights had been seemingly indifferent to their plays as books. At first the absence and later the inadequacy of copyright protection made actors and authors reluctant to publish an authorized text which might be used by stage rivals and other pirates. And it is always possible that the reading of a play may become a substitute for going to the theatre to see it acted. There were printed plays in plenty in Britain throughout the nineteenth century, but most of them were cheaply and unattractively produced in poor type on wretched paper and in flimsy covers. Moreover, little or no effort was made to assist the reader to visualize the author's intentions in regard to the acting and staging of his play. At best, and with such printed aids as the playwright may choose to give, the reading of plays requires an alert visual imagination, for the reader must stage the play in his own mind. From Shakespear's time until 1898, printed plays by British authors contained nothing but the stage dialogue—often far from accurate—and bare stage-directions for the players' exits and entrances, with, in some instances, a few words about scenery and costume, and an occasional hint for gesture, intonation, and emphasis. What Shaw desiderated in the printing of his plays was the incorporation of descriptive and explanatory matter which would help the reader to perceive the characters and their motives and circumstances as they had been imagined by the playwright. 'This', wrote Shaw,[1] 'means the institution of a new art; and I daresay that before these two volumes are ten years old, the bald attempt they make at it will be left far behind.' That prophecy was fairly accurate, for when in the 1910s J. M. Barrie published his own plays, dialogue and descriptive matter

[1] Preface to *Three Unpleasant Plays* (*Plays Pleasant and Unpleasant*, Vol. I, 1898), p. xxi.

were intermingled (see, e.g., *The Admirable Crichton*, first published in 1914). In the meantime Shaw's innovations had been adopted by other playwrights and a large play-reading public had been created. If the printed text of Pinero's *The Second Mrs Tanqueray* (published 1895) be compared with the Shaw volumes of 1898 the nature and extent of the innovations will be clearly seen. (It is of interest to note that in Shaw's first printed play—the Independent Theatre edition of *Widowers' Houses* (1893)—there is no descriptive elaboration such as he adopted five years later.) *Man and Superman* shows how far Shaw himself had progressed by 1903 in this transformation of printed plays.

In their contracts with authors it is usual for publishers to specify that they themselves decide and control all details of production (i.e. style of type and binding, quality and size of paper, number to be printed, and selling price). As the financial risk is taken by the publishers, these are reasonable conditions. The author customarily receives a royalty on each copy sold. At an early stage in his career as a playwright, however, Bernard Shaw undertook financial responsibility for his printed works, engaging printers and publishers as production and distribution agents, paying all costs and charges himself, and profiting by any balance. It was by adopting this method that he was able to ensure a consistent standard in the physical appearance and material quality of his books. While they reflect certain personal idiosyncrasies in presentation, they are, in their several editions and as a whole, the best designed and most orderly collection of volumes for which any modern author has been responsible. Shaw's talent for co-operation is shown by the fact, probably unique, that his printers remained unchanged from 1898, and his publishers from 1903, until the end of his life.[1]

[1] The printing history of Shaw's works was given in detail with many illustrations in a valuable article by James Shand—'Author and Printer: G.B.S. and R. & R. C[lark]: 1888-1948', *Alphabet and Image*, No. 8, London, December 1948, pp. 3-38—based largely upon information from the printers' managing director, Dr William Maxwell.

VII

Shaw died on 2 November 1950 at the age of ninety-four, leaving a fortune of £367,000. He had refused all offers of State honours, including the Order of Merit. As *Pygmalion* demonstrates, phonetics and the desirability of civilized pronunciation had long been one of his chief preoccupations, and his will directed that the first claim on his estate should be the cost of financing a reformed alphabet to consist of not fewer than forty characters, each character to represent one English spoken sound and one only. His aim was to establish an alphabet that would avoid combinations of characters for sounds that could be represented by single characters, thus saving time in writing and preventing the existing confusion caused by the frequent use of identical letters and letter-groups for dissimilar pronunciations (e.g. plough, rough, cough) and dissimilar spellings for similar pronunciations (tie, nigh, buy, rye). Since there was no practical outcome, an application made to the High Court in 1957 resulted in a judicial declaration that this provision in Shaw's will was invalid in law. Nevertheless, the three institutions (see below) that by Shaw's testamentary direction then became entitled to benefit, agreed to finance a competition for the designing of a new alphabet, and in January 1963 *Androcles and the Lion* was published in a forty-eight-character script designed by Kingsley Read.

During the intervening years the sum originally left by Shaw had been substantially increased to some half a million pounds by income accumulating from performing fees, sales of books, film rights, and a notably large increment from the adaption of *Pygmalion* as *My Fair Lady*, first as a musical play and then as a film.[1] The institutions Shaw nominated as residuary legatees are the National Gallery of Ireland (where he had acquired a fruitful knowledge of art in early years), the British Museum Reading Room (of

[1] It was announced (*The Times*, 8 February 1962) that the film rights had been bought for five-and-a-half million dollars (about £1,950,000).

which he had made constant use after reaching London), and the Royal Academy of Dramatic Art (which he had helped to found). All three institutions will continue to benefit from accruing royalties and fees until the Shaw copyrights expire in AD 2000.[1]

Although tendentious comment on Shaw continued in odd corners for some time after his death, his literary reputation slumped far less than is common in the decade after a great writer's work is ended. In his lifetime he had friends in every quarter, and the published memoirs of eminent contemporaries give abundant evidence of his personal integrity, kindliness, and generosity. His plays continue to be performed with success by professionals and amateurs alike, and in two directions his after-fame has grown: as a theatre critic and as a music critic he has soared in esteem. Moreover, his plays are repeatedly surprising audiences of the new generation by their 'topicality', for current modes and tendencies are found to have been often prefigured there (see above, pp. 7-8). But this is only to say that Shaw, like all truly great creative writers, was ahead of his age.

[1] But Shaw's letters and other writings first published after his death remain in copyright until fifty years after the date of publication. The Bodley Head edition of the plays, started in 1970, includes material not previously published (see Select Bibliography, p. 45).

FIRST PERFORMANCES OF SHAW'S PRINCIPAL PLAYS

Fuller details are given in Broad: *Dictionary to the Plays and Novels of Bernard Shaw*, 1929, and Colbourne: *The Real Bernard Shaw*, 1949. Before the British Copyright Act 1911, the protection given to plays was inadequate and uncertain, and dramatists sometimes took the precaution of arranging a 'copyright performance' in a public theatre. This might be no more than a public reading from the author's manuscript, with professional actors and actresses as readers, but without scenery or stage costume. Colbourne does not list such 'performances', but they are included by Broad.

When a first performance took place outside Britain, the date and place of the first British performance are also given below.

1892 (9 Dec.) *Widowers' Houses*, Independent Theatre Society, Royalty Theatre, London.

1894 (21 Apr.) *Arms and the Man*, Avenue Theatre, London.

1895 (30 Mar.) *Candida*, Theatre Royal, South Shields, Durham.

1897 (1 Oct.) *The Devil's Disciple*, Harmanns Bleeker Hall, Albany, New York, USA
Princess of Wales's Theatre, Kennington, London, 26 Sept. 1899.

1899 (26 Nov.) *You Never Can Tell*, Stage Society, Royalty Theatre, London.

1900 (16 Dec.) *Captain Brassbound's Conversion*, Stage Society, Strand Theatre, London.

1901 (1 May) *Caesar and Cleopatra*,[1] Fine Arts Building, Chicago, USA
Grand Theatre, Leeds, 16 Sept. 1907.

1902 (5 Jan.) *Mrs Warren's Profession*, Stage Society, New Lyric Theatre, London.

[1] The catalogue of the Exhibition Celebrating the 90th Birthday of Bernard Shaw, organized by the National Book League at 7 Albemarle Street, London, in July 1946 mentions a programme of a production of this play at the Fifth Avenue Theatre, New York, USA, in 1897; and also a playbill of a production at the Theatre Royal, Newcastle upon Tyne in 1899. The latter was a copyright performance with Mrs Patrick Campbell in the cast. The reference to an 1897 performance is baffling, for the play was not completed until 1898.

1904 (1 Nov.) *John Bull's Other Island*, Royal Court Theatre, London.

1905 (20 Feb.) *The Philanderer*, New Stage Club, Cripplegate Institute, London.

(21 May) *Man and Superman*, Royal Court Theatre, London. Act III, the scene in hell (usually omitted because of its length, though it is the most important of Shaw's writings up to that date), was first performed—as a separate one-act play—at the same theatre on 4 June 1907.

(28 Nov.) *Major Barbara*, Royal Court Theatre, London.

1906 (20 Nov.) *The Doctor's Dilemma*, Royal Court Theatre, London.

1908 (12 May) *Getting Married*, Theatre Royal, Haymarket, London.

1909 (25 Aug.) *The Shewing-up of Blanco Posnet*, Abbey Theatre, Dublin, Ireland.
Aldwych Theatre, London, 5 Dec. 1909.

1910 (23 Feb.) *Misalliance*, Duke of York's Theatre, London.

1911 (19 Apr.) *Fanny's First Play*, Little Theatre, London.

1912 (25 Nov.) *Androcles and the Lion*, Kleines Theatre, Berlin.
St James's Theatre, London, 1 Sept. 1913.

1913 (16 Oct.) *Pygmalion*, Hofburg Theatre, Vienna.
His Majesty's Theatre, London, 11 Apr. 1914.

1920 (10 Nov.) *Heartbreak House*, Theatre Guild, Garrick Theatre, New York, USA
Royal Court Theatre, London, 18 Oct. 1921.

1922 (27 Feb.)[1] *Back to Methuselah*, Theatre Guild, Garrick Theatre, New York, USA
Repertory Theatre, Birmingham, 9 Oct. 1923.

1923 (28 Dec.) *Saint Joan*, Theatre Guild, Garrick Theatre, New York, USA
New Theatre, London, 26 Mar. 1924.

[1] *Back to Methuselah* is a cycle of five plays. The whole cycle was given in both New York and Birmingham, but on varying dates. The dates given here relate to Part I.

1929 (14 June) *The Apple Cart*, Polish Theatre, Warsaw.
Malvern Festival,[1] 19 Aug. 1929.

1932 (23 Feb.) *Too True to be Good*, New York Theatre Guild, Colonial Theatre, Boston, USA
Malvern Festival, 6 Aug. 1932.

1933 (25 Nov.) *On the Rocks*, Winter Garden Theatre, London.

1936 (4 Jan.) *The Millionairess*, Academy Theatre, Vienna.
De la Warr Pavilion, Bexhill, 17 Nov. 1936.

1938 (1 Aug.) *Geneva*, Malvern Festival.

1939 (12 Aug.) *In Good King Charles's Golden Days*, Malvern Festival.

1948 (21 Oct.) *Buoyant Billions*. Schauspielhaus, Zurich.
Malvern Festival, 13 Aug. 1949.

[1] The Malvern Festival, in Worcestershire, England, was founded in 1929 by Sir Barry Jackson (of the Birmingham Repertory Theatre) in honour of Bernard Shaw. In later years plays from several centuries were performed. The Festival was suspended when the Second World War began, but at a resumption in 1949 Shaw's *Buoyant Billions* was given.

BERNARD SHAW

A Select Bibliography

(Place of publication London, unless stated otherwise)

Bibliography:

'A Bibliography of the Books and Pamphlets of George Bernard Shaw', by G. H. Wells. Supplement to *The Bookman's Journal*, Feb., Apr. 1925; revised and enlarged, third series, Vol. XVI, viii, 1928.

DICTIONARY TO THE PLAYS AND NOVELS OF BERNARD SHAW, WITH BIBLIOGRAPHY OF HIS WORKS AND OF THE LITERATURE CONCERNING HIM, WITH A RECORD OF THE PRINCIPAL SHAVIAN PLAY PRODUCTIONS by C. L. and V. M. Broad (1929).

THE HISTORY OF A FAMOUS NOVEL [An Unsocial Socialist], by F. E. Loewenstein (1946).

THE REHEARSAL COPIES OF BERNARD SHAW'S PLAYS, by F. E. Loewenstein (1950).

Collected Editions:

THE COLLECTED EDITION, 30 vols (1930-2)

—limited to 1,000 numbered sets. Three additional volumes were published later. Some material afterwards included in the Standard Edition does not appear in the Collected Edition.

THE STANDARD EDITION, 36 vols (1931-50)

—this was the only inclusive edition.

COMPLETE PLAYS (1931)

—enlarged editions 1934, 1938, and 1950.

COMPLETE PREFACES (1934)

—enlarged edition, 1938.

THE PENGUIN EDITION, 10 vols (1946: additional volumes later)

—ten volumes were issued on the author's ninetieth birthday; an eleventh in his centenary year.

THE BODLEY HEAD BERNARD SHAW. Vol. I, *etc.* (1970-)

—Vol. I contains the seven plays originally published, 1898, as 'Plays Unpleasant' and 'Plays Pleasant' with the Prefaces. (Under the editorial supervision of Professor Dan H. Laurence, this definitive Bodley Head edition, when complete, will contain in six or seven volumes Shaw's fifty-two plays, with all his Prefaces, revisions and corrections, and pertinent essays and programme notes by the author, as well as hitherto unpublished material. A history of composition, publication, and earliest performances is provided for each play, and a cast of characters.)

Separate Works:

CASHEL BYRON'S PROFESSION (1886). *Novel*

AN UNSOCIAL SOCIALIST (1887). *Novel*

THE QUINTESSENCE OF IBSENISM (1891). *Criticism*
—enlarged edition (completed to the death of Ibsen), 1913. In the Standard Edition this appeared in *Major Critical Essays.*

WIDOWERS' HOUSES (1893). Being Number One of the Independent Theatre Series of Plays, ed. J. T. Grein. *Drama*
—this was the first play by Shaw to appear in print. It was later included in Vol. I of *Plays Pleasant and Unpleasant* (1898).

THE IMPOSSIBILITIES OF ANARCHISM (1893). *Political*
—Fabian Tract No. 45. In the Standard Edition this appeared in *Essays in Fabian Socialism.*

THE PERFECT WAGNERITE: A Commentary on *The Ring of the Nibelungs* (1898; 3rd edition 1913). *Criticism*
—in the Standard Edition this appeared in *Major Critical Essays.*

PLAYS PLEASANT AND UNPLEASANT, 2 vols (1898). *Drama*
PLAYS UNPLEASANT contains: Preface: Mainly About Myself; 'Widowers' Houses: A Play'; 'The Philanderer: A Topical Comedy', with a Prefatory Note; 'Mrs Warren's Profession: A Play', with a Preface
—separate edition of 'Mrs Warren's Profession', with an Apology (1903).

PLAYS PLEASANT contains: Preface, 'Arms and the Man: An Anti-Romantic Comedy'; 'Candida: A Mystery'; 'The Man of Destiny: A Fictitious Paragraph of History'; 'You Never Can Tell: A Comedy'.

LOVE AMONG THE ARTISTS; Chicago (1900). *Novel*

THREE PLAYS FOR PURITANS (1901). *Drama*
—contains: Preface: Why for Puritans? On Diabolonian Ethics. Better than Shakespear?; 'The Devil's Disciple: A Melodrama', with Notes on General Burgoyne and on Brudenell; 'Caesar and Cleopatra: A History', with Notes on Cleopatra's Cure for Baldness, Apparent Anachronisms, Cleopatra, Britannus and Julius Caesar; 'Captain Brassbound's Conversion: An Adventure', with Notes on the Sources of the Play, and on English and American Dialects.

MAN AND SUPERMAN (1903). *Drama*
—contains: 'Man and Superman: A Comedy and a Philosophy', with an Epistle Dedicatory to A. B. Walkley. The play is followed by 'The Revolutionist's Handbook and Pocket Companion by John Tanner, MIRC (Member of the Idle Rich Class)' [*John Tanner is the leading male character in 'Man and Superman'*], to which is appended Maxims for Revolutionists.

THE COMMON SENSE OF MUNICIPAL TRADING (1904). *Sociology*
—in the Standard Edition this appeared in *Essays in Fabian Socialism.*

PASSION, POISON, AND PETRIFACTION (1905). *Drama*
—first published in Furniss's Xmas Annual, 1905.

THE IRRATIONAL KNOT (1905). *Novel*

DRAMATIC OPINIONS AND ESSAYS: With an Apology [by the author]. Containing as well a Word on the Dramatic Opinions and Essays of Bernard Shaw by James Huneker, 2 vols; New York (1906), London (1907). *Criticism*
—this was a selection made by Huneker from Shaw's articles in *The Saturday Review*, all of which were afterwards included in *Our Theatres in the Nineties*, 3 vols (Collected Edition 1931; Standard Edition, 1932).

JOHN BULL'S OTHER ISLAND (1907). *Drama*
—contains: 'John Bull's Other Island', with a Preface for Politicians; 'How He Lied to Her Husband', with a Prefatory Note; 'Major Barbara', with a Preface: First Aid to Critics.

THE SANITY OF ART: An Exposure of the Current Nonsense about Artists being Degenerate (1908). *Criticism*
—a critical reply to Max Nordau's *Entartung*. In the Standard Edition this appeared in *Major Critical Essays.*

PRESS CUTTINGS: A Topical Sketch compiled from the Editorial and Correspondence Columns of the Daily Papers during the Women's War in 1909 (1909). *Drama*
—in the Standard Edition this appeared in *Translations and Tomfooleries*, 1926.

BRIEUX: A Preface (1910). *Criticism*
—a consideration of the work of the French playwright Eugène Brieux, author of 'Damaged Goods', etc. The preface was incorporated in 1911 in an English edition of *Three Plays by Brieux.*

THE DOCTOR'S DILEMMA (1911). *Drama*

—contains: 'The Doctor's Dilemma: A Tragedy', with a Preface on Doctors; 'Getting Married: A Comedy', with a Preface on the Revolt against Marriage; 'The Shewing-up of Blanco Posnet: A Melodrama', with a Preface on the Censorship.

MISALLIANCE (1914). *Drama*

—contains: 'Misalliance', with a Prefatory Treatise on Parents and Children; 'The Dark Lady of the Sonnets', with a Preface on How the Play came to be Written; 'Fanny's First Play: An Easy Play for a Little Theatre', with a Preface.

COMMON SENSE ABOUT THE WAR (1914). *Political*

—included as a 24-page supplement with the *New Statesman*, 14 November 1914. In the Standard Edition this appeared in *What I Really Wrote about the War*, 1931.

ANDROCLES AND THE LION (1916). *Drama*

—contains: 'Androcles and the Lion: a Fable Play', with a Preface on the Prospects of Christianity; 'Overruled', with a Preface on the Alleviations of Monogamy; 'Pygmalion: A Romance in Five Acts', with a Preface on a Professor of Phonetics [Henry Sweet] and a Sequel [*telling the rest of the story in narrative after the play ends*], What Happened Afterwards.

HEARTBREAK HOUSE (1919). *Drama*

—contains: 'Heartbreak House: A Fantasia in the Russian Manner on English Themes', with a Preface on Heartbreak House and Horseback Hall; 'Great Catherine (Whom Glory still Adores)', with a Preface: The Author's Apology for Great Catherine; 'Playlets of the War': 'O'Flaherty, V.C.: A Recruiting Pamphlet', with a Preface; 'The Inca of Perusalem: An Almost Historical Comedietta', with a Preface; 'Augustus does his Bit: A True-to-Life Farce', with a Prefatory Note; 'Annajanska, The Bolshevik Empress: a Revolutionary Romancelet', with a Prefatory Note.

BACK TO METHUSELAH (1921). *Drama*

—contains: 'Back to Methuselah: A Metabiological Pentateuch' [*in five parts*, In the Beginning, The Gospel of the Brothers Barnabas, The Thing Happens, Tragedy of an Elderly Gentleman, As Far As Thought can Reach], with a Preface on The Infidel Half-Century. A revised edition with a new Postscript was issued as No. 500 in The World's Classics, 1946.

SAINT JOAN: A Chronicle Play in Six Scenes and an Epilogue, with a Preface (1924). *Drama*

TRANSLATIONS AND TOMFOOLERIES (1926). *Drama*
—contains: 'Jitta's Atonement', from the German of Siegfried Trebitsch, with a Translator's Note; 'Trifles and Tomfooleries'; 'The Admirable Bashville, or, Constancy Unrewarded': Being the Novel of Cashel Byron's Profession done into a Stage Play in Three Acts and in Blank Verse, with a Preface; 'Press Cuttings: A Topical Sketch compiled from the Editorial and Correspondence Columns of the Daily Papers during the Women's War in 1909'; 'The Glimpse of Reality: A Tragedietta'; 'Passion, Poison, and Petrifaction, or, The Fatal Gazogene: a Brief Tragedy for Barns and Booths', with a Prefatory Note; 'The Fascinating Foundling: A Disgrace to the Author'; 'The Music-Cure: A Piece of Utter Nonsense', with a Prefatory Note.

THE INTELLIGENT WOMAN'S GUIDE TO SOCIALISM AND CAPITALISM (1928). *Political*

THE LEAGUE OF NATIONS (1920). *Political*
—Fabian Tract No. 226. In the Standard Edition this appeared in *What I Really Wrote about the War*, 1931.

THE APPLE CART: A Political Extravanganza, with a Preface (1930). *Drama*

IMMATURITY (1930). *Novel*
—Shaw's first novel, written in 1879. First published in 1930 in the Collected Edition, with a Preface dated 1921.

MAJOR CRITICAL ESSAYS (1930)
—contains: 'The Quintessence of Ibsenism'; 'The Perfect Wagnerite'; 'The Sanity of Art'.

OUR THEATRES IN THE NINETIES, 3 vols (1931)
—contains theatre criticism contributed week by week to *The Saturday Review*, from 5 January 1895 to 21 May 1898. See page 47 above, *Dramatic Opinions and Essays* (1906).

WHAT I REALLY WROTE ABOUT THE WAR (1931).

MUSIC IN LONDON 1890–94, 3 vols (1931)
—contains criticism contributed week by week to *The World*, from 28 May 1890 to 8 August 1894.

DOCTORS' DELUSIONS; CRUDE CRIMINOLOGY; SHAM EDUCATION (1931). *Sociology*

PEN PORTRAITS AND REVIEWS (1931). *Criticism*

THE ADVENTURES OF THE BLACK GIRL IN HER SEARCH FOR GOD (1932). *Short Story*
—in the Standard Edition this appeared in *The Black Girl and Some Lesser Tales*, 1934.

ESSAYS IN FABIAN SOCIALISM (1932). *Political*

SHORT STORIES (1932)
—reprinted together with *The Adventures of the Black Girl in her Search for God* in the Standard Edition, 1934.

THE FUTURE OF POLITICAL SCIENCE IN AMERICA: An Address by Mr Bernard Shaw to the Academy of Political Science at the Metropolitan Opera House, New York, on 11 April 1933; New York (1933).
—the English edition, 1933, was titled *The Political Madhouse in America and Nearer Home, with an Explanation.*

TOO TRUE TO BE GOOD (1934). *Drama*
—contains: 'Too True to be Good: A Political Extravaganza', with a Preface; 'Village Wooing: A Comediettina for Two Voices'; 'On the Rocks: A Political Comedy', with a Preface.

THE BLACK GIRL AND SOME LESSER TALES (first titled SHORT STORIES, SCRAPS AND SHAVINGS) (1934).

THE SIMPLETON OF THE UNEXPECTED ISLES (1936). *Drama*
—contains: 'The Simpleton of the Unexpected Isles: A Vision of Judgment', with a Preface on Days of Judgment; 'The Six of Calais: A Medieval War Story by Jean Froissart, Auguste Rodin, and Bernard Shaw', with a Prefatory to the Six of Calais; 'The Millionairess: Comedy in Four Acts', with a Preface on Bosses.

LONDON MUSIC IN 1888-89 AS HEARD BY CORNO DI BASSETTO (LATER KNOWN AS BERNARD SHAW) WITH SOME FURTHER AUTOBIOGRAPHICAL PARTICULARS (1937). *Criticism*

GENEVA: A Fancied Page of History, in Three Acts (1939). *Drama*
—re-issued with a new act in the Standard Edition, 1946.

IN GOOD KING CHARLES'S GOLDEN DAYS: A History Lesson (1939). *Drama*

SHAW GIVES HIMSELF AWAY: An Autobiographical Miscellany (1939). *Autobiography*

—300 copies published by the Gregynog Press. With the exception of the prefaces to *Immaturity* and to *The Irrational Knot* (which appeared in the Standard Edition in the novels bearing those titles) and of 'Bits and Scraps' (fragments from various works by Shaw), the material in this volume was reprinted in *Sixteen Self Sketches*, 1949.

EVERYBODY'S POLITICAL WHAT'S WHAT (1944). *Political*

GENEVA; CYMBELINE REFINISHED; GOOD KING CHARLES (1946). *Drama*

—contains: Preface to 'Geneva'; 'Geneva: Another Political Extravaganza'; Foreword to 'Cymbeline Refinished'; 'Cymbeline Refinished: A variation on Shakespear's Ending'; Preface to 'Good King Charles'; 'In Good King Charles's Golden Days: A True History that Never Happened'.

SIXTEEN SELF SKETCHES (1949). *Autobiography*

—contains: I. My First Biographer [*extracts from his father's letters to his mother*, 1857]; II. My Apology for this Book; III. My Mother and Her Relatives; IV. Shame and Wounded Snobbery; V. My Office-Boyhood; VI. End of a Clerk in Dublin; VII. Nine Years of Failure as a Novelist Ending in Success as Critic; VIII. In the Days of My Youth; IX. Who I am, and what I think; X. How I became a Public Speaker; XI. Fruitful Friendships; XII. Am I an Educated Person?; XIII. What is My Religious Faith?; XIV. Biographers' Blunders Corrected; XV. Origin of Corno di Bassetto; XVI. To Frank Harris on Sex in Biography; XVII. How Frank ought to have done it; Envoy.

BUOYANT BILLIONS (1950). *Drama*

—limited edition, with illustrations by Clare Winsten.

BERNARD SHAW'S RHYMING PICTURE GUIDE TO AYOT SAINT LAWRENCE; Luton (1950). *Topography*

BUOYANT BILLIONS (1951). *Drama*

—Standard Edition. Contains: 'Buoyant Billions', 'Farfetched Fables', and 'Shakes verses Shav' with Prefaces.

MY DEAR DOROTHEA (1956)

—not previously published, but written in 1877 (when Shaw was twenty-one) as an open letter to a child outlining 'a practical system of moral education for females'.

ANDROCLES AND THE LION (1963). *Drama*
—the Shaw Alphabet Edition.

SIX PLAYS (1963)
—contains 'Arms and the Man', 'Man and Superman'; 'Major Barbara'; 'Pygmalion'; 'Heartbreak House'; 'Saint Joan'.

THE DEVIL'S DISCIPLE; MAJOR BARBARA; SAINT JOAN (1966)
—Everyman's Library.

Letters:

LETTERS FROM GEORGE BERNARD SHAW TO MISS ALMA MURRAY; Edinburgh (1927)
—only thirty copies printed for private circulation.

ELLEN TERRY AND BERNARD SHAW: A Correspondence, ed. Christopher St John, with a Preface by Bernard Shaw (1930).

FLORENCE FARR, BERNARD SHAW, AND W. B. YEATS, ed. Clifford Bax; Dublin (1941)
—limited edition. Ordinary edition, 1946.

BERNARD SHAW AND MRS PATRICK CAMPBELL: Their Correspondence, ed. Alan Dent (1952).

BERNARD SHAW'S LETTERS TO GRANVILLE BARKER, ed. C. B. Purdom (1957).

TO A YOUNG ACTRESS: The letters of Bernard Shaw to Molly Tompkins, 1921-1949, ed. P. Tompkins (1960).

COLLECTED LETTERS, ed. Dan H. Laucrene, Vol. I, 1874-1897 (1965).

Posthumously Collected Writings and Speeches:

HOW TO BECOME A MUSICAL CRITIC: Hitherto uncollected writings, ed. Dan H. Laurence (1960)
—'A survey of Shaw's unreprinted opinions of music covering a period of three-quarters of a century from 1876 to 1950.'

PLATFORM AND PULPIT: Hitherto uncollected material, ed. Dan H. Laurence (1962)
—'The full texts of more than thirty of Shaw's formal lectures, extemporary speeches, and debates, covering the period from 1885 to 1946.'

THE MATTER WITH IRELAND: Hitherto uncollected writings, ed. David H. Greene and Dan H. Laurence (1962)
—'Fifty essays written between 1886 and 1950' on Irish problems and persons.

Selections:

SELECTED PASSAGES FROM THE WORKS OF BERNARD SHAW, chosen by Charlotte F. Shaw [Mrs Bernard Shaw] (1912).

THE QUINTESSENCE OF G.B.S., with a commentary by Stephen Winsten (1949)
—an anthology of extracts.

PLAYS AND PLAYERS: Essays on the Theatre, selected by A. C. Ward (1952).

SELECTED PROSE OF BERNARD SHAW, chosen and edited by Diarmuid Russell; New York (1952), London (1953).

SHAW ON MUSIC: A selection from the Music Criticism of Bernard Shaw, ed. Eric Bentley (1955).

SHAW ON THEATRE, ed. E. J. West (1958)
—'Fifty years of essays, letters and articles collected for the first time in book form.'

BERNARD SHAW: A Prose Anthology. Passages selected, with an Introduction and Notes, by H. M. Burton. Preface by A. C. Ward
—this anthology draws upon the whole range of Shaw's works: plays, prefaces, music and drama criticism, political writings, essays, and fiction (1959).

SHAW ON SHAKESPEARE: An Anthology of Bernard Shaw's writings on the Plays and Production of Shakespeare, ed. Edwin Wilson (1961).

SHAW: An Autobiography 1856-1898. Selected by Stanley Weintraub from Bernard Shaw's prefaces, reviews, speeches and other sources (1970).

Adaptations:

MY FAIR LADY. A Musical Play in Two Acts based on *Pygmalion* by Bernard Shaw. Adaptation and lyrics by A. J. Lerner. Illustrated by Cecil Beaton (1958).

DEAR LIAR: A Comedy of Letters. Adapted by Jerome Kilty from the Correspondence of Bernard Shaw and Mrs Patrick Campbell (1960).

Some Critical and Biographical Studies:

GEORGE BERNARD SHAW: HIS PLAYS, by H. L. Mencken (1905).

BERNARD SHAW, by Holbrook Jackson (1907).

GEORGE BERNARD SHAW, by G. K. Chesterton, 1910 [1909]
—new edition with additional chapter, 1935.

GEORGE BERNARD SHAW: HIS LIFE AND WORKS. A CRITICAL BIOGRAPHY, by Archibald Henderson (1911)
—new edition 1932.

LE MOLIÈRE DU XXe SIÈCLE: BERNARD SHAW, by A. F. A. Hamon; Paris (1913) [1912]
—English translation by Eden and Cedar Paul, 1915.

THE QUINTESSENCE OF BERNARD SHAW, by H. C. Duffin (1920)
—revised and enlarged edition 1939.

SHAW, by J. S. Collis (1925).

THE REAL BERNARD SHAW, by Maurice Colbourne (1930)
—new edition, re-written 1939. Enlarged edition, 1949.

ELLEN TERRY AND HER SECRET SELF, by E. Gordon Craig (1931).

FRANK HARRIS ON BERNARD SHAW: An Unauthorised Biography based on Firsthand Information, with a Postscript by Mr Shaw (1931).

BERNARD SHAW: HIS LIFE AND PERSONALITY, by Hesketh Pearson (1942).

G.B.S. 90: ASPECTS OF BERNARD SHAW'S LIFE AND WORKS, ed. Stephen Winsten (1946)
—published in commemoration of Shaw's 90th birthday with contributions by Gilbert Murray, John Masefield, Lord Passfield (Sidney Webb), H. G. Wells, Sir Max Beerbohm, James Bridie, Lord Dunsany, Lord Keynes, W. R. Inge, Kenneth Barnes, Aldous Huxley, and seventeen others.

BERNARD SHAW, by Eric Bentley; New York (1947), London (new edition, 1967).

SHAW, by C. E. M. Joad (1949).

30 YEARS WITH G.B.S., by Blanche Patch (1951).

G.B.S.: A POSTSCRIPT, by Hesketh Pearson (1951).

BERNARD SHAW, by A. C. Ward (1951).

BERNARD SHAW: A CHRONICLE, by R. F. Rattray (1951).

BERNARD SHAW: HIS LIFE, WORK AND FRIENDS, by St John Ervine (1956)
—the definitive biography.

GEORGE BERNARD SHAW: MAN OF THE CENTURY, by Archibald Henderson; New York (1956).

BERNARD SHAW: HIS LIFE AND PERSONALITY, by Hesketh Pearson (1961)
—a combined edition of the 1942 volume with the same title and *G.B.S.: A Postscript* (1951) and including 'a few episodes which for one reason or another were omitted' in 1942.

'The Nun and the Dramatist', by a Nun of Stanbrook, *Cornhill Magazine*, No. 1008, Summer 1956.
—an account, with the letters that passed between them, of the 'astonishingly candid friendship' between Shaw and Dame Laurentia McLachlan, Abbess of Stanbrook.

MRS G.B.S.: A BIOGRAPHICAL PORTRAIT OF CHARLOTTE SHAW, by Janet Dunbar (1963).

PRIVATE SHAW AND PUBLIC SHAW, by Stanley Weintraub (1962)
—an account of the literary friendship of T. E. Lawrence and Shaw.

G.B.S. AND THE LUNATIC, by Lawrence Langner (1963)
—an account of the New York Theatre Guild Shaw productions.

A SHAVIAN GUIDE TO THE INTELLIGENT WOMAN, by Barbara Bellow Watson (1964).

GEORGE BERNARD SHAW ON LANGUAGE, ed. Abraham Tauber with a Foreword by Sir James Pitman (1965).

SHAW IN HIS TIME, by Ivor Brown (1965).

SHAW AND THE CHARLATAN GENIUS, by John O'Donovan (1965)
—a memoir of G. J. Vandeleur Lee.

THE UNREPENTANT PILGRIM, by J. Percy Smith (1966)
—a record of Shaw's progress to his personal form of belief.

BERNARD SHAW: A REASSESSMENT, by Colin Wilson (1969).

BERNARD SHAW AND THE ART OF DESTROYING IDEALS: The Early Plays, by Charles A. Carpenter (1970).

Miscellaneous:

BERNARD SHAW THROUGH THE CAMERA
—238 Photographs, including many taken by Mr Shaw, selected and introduced by F. E. Loewenstein (1948).

THEATRICAL COMPANION TO SHAW. A Pictorial Record of the First Performances of the Plays, by Raymond Mander and Joe Mitchenson. Introduction by Sir Barry Jackson (1956).

SHAW THE VILLAGER AND HUMAN BEING: A Biographical Symposium. Narrated and Edited by Allan Chappelow. Foreword by Dame Sybil Thorndike (1961)
—personal opinions of Shaw collected by the author, mainly through conversations with men and women living in the village of Ayot St Lawrence, Hertfordshire; with many illustrations.

BERNARD SHAW: A Pictorial Biography, by Margaret Shenfield (1962).

Note: Shaw's influential services for the Fabian Society in its early years are surveyed in *The Story of Fabian Socialism* by M. Cole (1961) and *Fabian Socialism and English Politics, 1884-1918* by A. M. McBriar (1962); and his association with *The New Statesman* in the *History of the 'New Statesman'* by Edward Hyams (1963).

INDEX OF PRINCIPAL PLAYS

(The title in italics refers to the volume in which the play appeared in the Standard Edition)

INDEX OF PRINCIPAL TITLED PREFACES

(The title in italics refers to the volume in which the preface originally appeared)

INDEX OF MISCELLANEOUS ESSAYS

(The title in italics refers to the volume in the Standard Edition in which the Essay appeared)